50 Delicious Pasta Recipes

By: Kelly Johnson

Table of Contents

- Spaghetti Carbonara
- Fettuccine Alfredo
- Penne Arrabbiata
- Lasagna Bolognese
- Pesto Genovese
- Spaghetti Aglio e Olio
- Rigatoni alla Norma
- Cacio e Pepe
- Tagliatelle al Ragù
- Orecchiette with Broccoli Rabe
- Linguine alle Vongole
- Macaroni and Cheese
- Tortellini in Brodo
- Baked Ziti
- Farfalle with Creamy Mushroom Sauce
- Fusilli with Sun-Dried Tomatoes
- Spaghetti Puttanesca

- Penne alla Vodka
- Gnocchi with Sage Butter
- Angel Hair with Garlic and Olive Oil
- Ravioli with Spinach and Ricotta
- Bucatini all'Amatriciana
- Pasta Primavera
- Cannelloni Stuffed with Ricotta and Spinach
- Lasagne Verde
- Spaghetti with Meatballs
- Orecchiette with Sausage and Peppers
- Rigatoni with Sausage and Broccoli
- Tagliatelle al Tartufo
- Gemelli with Pesto and Potatoes
- Linguine with Clams
- Rotini with Roasted Vegetables
- Capellini with Lemon and Basil
- Manicotti with Meat Sauce
- Penne with Gorgonzola Cream Sauce
- Spaghetti with Crab and Chili

- Fettuccine with Lobster Sauce
- Lasagna Primavera
- Pappardelle with Rabbit Ragù
- Pasta Salad with Italian Dressing
- Ravioli with Sage Butter and Parmesan
- Bucatini with Pancetta and Peas
- Spaghetti with Garlic and Breadcrumbs
- Penne with Eggplant and Tomato Sauce
- Gnocchi alla Sorrentina
- Cavatappi with Cheddar and Bacon
- Tagliolini with Lemon and Parmesan
- Tortellini with Creamy Mushroom Sauce
- Fusilli with Pesto and Pine Nuts
- Spaghetti with Anchovies and Capers

Spaghetti Carbonara

Ingredients:

- 12 oz spaghetti
- 4 oz pancetta or guanciale, diced
- 2 large eggs
- 1 cup grated Pecorino Romano or Parmesan
- 2 cloves garlic, peeled
- Freshly ground black pepper
- Salt

Instructions:

1. Cook spaghetti in salted boiling water until al dente.
2. In a pan, sauté pancetta with garlic until crispy, then remove garlic.
3. Beat eggs and cheese together in a bowl.
4. Drain pasta, reserving some pasta water.
5. Toss pasta quickly with pancetta off the heat.
6. Stir in egg and cheese mixture, adding pasta water to create a creamy sauce.
7. Season generously with black pepper and serve immediately.

Fettuccine Alfredo

Ingredients:

- 12 oz fettuccine
- 1 cup heavy cream
- ½ cup unsalted butter
- 1 cup grated Parmesan
- Salt and pepper

Instructions:

1. Cook fettuccine in salted water until al dente.
2. In a saucepan, melt butter and add cream, simmer gently.
3. Stir in Parmesan until melted and sauce thickens.
4. Toss pasta in sauce, season with salt and pepper. Serve warm.

Penne Arrabbiata

Ingredients:

- 12 oz penne pasta
- 3 tbsp olive oil
- 3 cloves garlic, minced
- 1 tsp red pepper flakes
- 1 can (14 oz) crushed tomatoes
- Salt and pepper
- Fresh parsley, chopped

Instructions:

1. Cook penne in salted water until al dente.
2. Heat olive oil, sauté garlic and red pepper flakes briefly.
3. Add crushed tomatoes, simmer 10-15 minutes.
4. Season with salt and pepper.
5. Toss pasta with sauce and sprinkle with parsley.

Lasagna Bolognese

Ingredients:

- Lasagna noodles
- 2 cups Bolognese sauce (meat ragù)
- 2 cups béchamel sauce
- 2 cups shredded mozzarella
- 1 cup grated Parmesan

Instructions:

1. Preheat oven to 375°F (190°C).
2. Cook noodles according to package.
3. Layer lasagna: ragù, noodles, béchamel, mozzarella, repeat ending with Parmesan.
4. Bake 35-40 minutes until bubbly and golden. Let rest before serving.

Pesto Genovese

Ingredients:

- 2 cups fresh basil leaves
- ½ cup pine nuts
- 2 cloves garlic
- ½ cup grated Parmesan
- 2/3 cup olive oil
- Salt

Instructions:

1. Blend basil, pine nuts, garlic, and Parmesan in a food processor.
2. Slowly add olive oil until smooth.
3. Toss with cooked pasta and serve.

Spaghetti Aglio e Olio

Ingredients:

- 12 oz spaghetti
- 6 cloves garlic, thinly sliced
- ½ cup olive oil
- 1 tsp red pepper flakes
- Fresh parsley, chopped
- Salt

Instructions:

1. Cook spaghetti until al dente.
2. Heat olive oil, sauté garlic until golden but not burnt.
3. Add red pepper flakes.
4. Toss pasta in garlic oil, season with salt, sprinkle parsley, serve.

Rigatoni alla Norma

Ingredients:

- 12 oz rigatoni
- 1 large eggplant, cubed
- 2 cups tomato sauce
- 1 cup ricotta salata or ricotta cheese
- 3 cloves garlic, minced
- Olive oil
- Fresh basil
- Salt and pepper

Instructions:

1. Salt eggplant cubes and let sit 30 mins, rinse and dry.
2. Fry eggplant in olive oil until golden.
3. Sauté garlic, add tomato sauce, simmer.
4. Cook rigatoni, toss with sauce and eggplant.
5. Serve topped with ricotta and basil.

Cacio e Pepe

Ingredients:

- 12 oz spaghetti or tonnarelli
- 1 ½ cups Pecorino Romano, grated
- 2 tsp freshly ground black pepper
- Salt

Instructions:

1. Cook pasta until al dente, reserving pasta water.
2. Toast pepper in a dry pan.
3. Toss hot pasta with cheese and pepper, adding pasta water gradually to make a creamy sauce.
4. Serve immediately.

Tagliatelle al Ragù

Ingredients:

- 12 oz tagliatelle
- 2 cups ragù (slow-cooked meat sauce)
- Grated Parmesan

Instructions:

1. Cook tagliatelle until al dente.
2. Heat ragù sauce.
3. Toss pasta with ragù, top with Parmesan.

Orecchiette with Broccoli Rabe

Ingredients:

- 12 oz orecchiette pasta
- 1 bunch broccoli rabe, trimmed and chopped
- 3 cloves garlic, sliced
- ¼ cup olive oil
- Red pepper flakes (optional)
- Salt and pepper
- Grated Pecorino Romano

Instructions:

1. Blanch broccoli rabe in boiling salted water for 2-3 minutes, drain.
2. Cook orecchiette in the same water until al dente.
3. Heat olive oil, sauté garlic and red pepper flakes.
4. Add broccoli rabe, cook 2-3 minutes, season with salt and pepper.
5. Toss pasta with broccoli rabe mixture, top with Pecorino Romano.

Linguine alle Vongole

Ingredients:

- 12 oz linguine
- 2 lbs fresh clams, scrubbed
- 4 cloves garlic, minced
- ½ cup white wine
- ¼ cup olive oil
- Red pepper flakes
- Fresh parsley, chopped
- Salt

Instructions:

1. Cook linguine until al dente.
2. Heat olive oil, sauté garlic and red pepper flakes.
3. Add clams and white wine, cover and cook until clams open.
4. Toss pasta with clams and sauce, sprinkle parsley, serve.

Macaroni and Cheese

Ingredients:

- 12 oz elbow macaroni
- 3 cups shredded cheddar cheese
- 2 cups milk
- 3 tbsp butter
- 3 tbsp flour
- Salt and pepper
- Optional: breadcrumbs for topping

Instructions:

1. Cook macaroni until al dente.
2. Make a roux: melt butter, whisk in flour until smooth.
3. Gradually add milk, whisk until thickened.
4. Stir in cheese until melted, season.
5. Mix sauce with pasta, bake with breadcrumbs at 350°F for 20 mins (optional).

Tortellini in Brodo

Ingredients:

- 12 oz fresh tortellini (cheese or meat-filled)
- 4 cups chicken broth
- Grated Parmesan
- Fresh parsley

Instructions:

1. Bring broth to a simmer.
2. Add tortellini, cook until they float.
3. Serve in bowls with broth, topped with Parmesan and parsley.

Baked Ziti

Ingredients:

- 12 oz ziti pasta
- 2 cups marinara sauce
- 2 cups shredded mozzarella
- 1 cup ricotta cheese
- ½ cup grated Parmesan

Instructions:

1. Cook pasta until al dente.
2. Mix pasta with marinara and ricotta.
3. Place in baking dish, top with mozzarella and Parmesan.
4. Bake at 375°F for 25-30 minutes until bubbly.

Farfalle with Creamy Mushroom Sauce

Ingredients:

- 12 oz farfalle
- 2 cups mushrooms, sliced
- 1 cup heavy cream
- 2 cloves garlic, minced
- 2 tbsp butter
- Salt and pepper
- Parsley for garnish

Instructions:

1. Cook farfalle until al dente.
2. Sauté mushrooms and garlic in butter until soft.
3. Add cream, simmer to thicken.
4. Toss pasta in sauce, season and garnish with parsley.

Fusilli with Sun-Dried Tomatoes

Ingredients:

- 12 oz fusilli
- ½ cup sun-dried tomatoes, chopped
- 3 cloves garlic, minced
- ¼ cup olive oil
- 1 tsp chili flakes (optional)
- Fresh basil
- Salt and pepper

Instructions:

1. Cook fusilli until al dente.
2. Sauté garlic and chili flakes in olive oil.
3. Add sun-dried tomatoes, cook 2 minutes.
4. Toss pasta with sauce, season, garnish with basil.

Spaghetti Puttanesca

Ingredients:

- 12 oz spaghetti
- 3 tbsp olive oil
- 3 cloves garlic, minced
- 1 can (14 oz) diced tomatoes
- ¼ cup Kalamata olives, pitted and sliced
- 2 tbsp capers
- ½ tsp red pepper flakes
- Fresh parsley
- Salt and pepper

Instructions:

1. Cook spaghetti until al dente.
2. Heat olive oil, sauté garlic and red pepper flakes.
3. Add tomatoes, olives, capers, simmer 10 minutes.
4. Toss pasta with sauce, garnish with parsley.

Penne alla Vodka

Ingredients:

- 12 oz penne
- 3 tbsp olive oil
- 1 small onion, finely chopped
- 2 cloves garlic, minced
- ½ cup vodka
- 1 can (14 oz) crushed tomatoes
- 1 cup heavy cream
- Salt and pepper
- Fresh basil

Instructions:

1. Cook penne until al dente.
2. Sauté onion and garlic in olive oil until soft.
3. Add vodka, cook off alcohol for 2 minutes.
4. Stir in tomatoes, simmer 10 minutes.
5. Add cream, season.
6. Toss pasta with sauce, garnish with basil.

Gnocchi with Sage Butter

Ingredients:

- 1 lb potato gnocchi
- 6 tbsp unsalted butter
- 8-10 fresh sage leaves
- Salt and pepper
- Grated Parmesan

Instructions:

1. Cook gnocchi in boiling salted water until they float. Drain.
2. In a pan, melt butter over medium heat, add sage leaves and cook until butter browns slightly and sage is crispy.
3. Toss gnocchi in sage butter, season with salt and pepper.
4. Serve topped with grated Parmesan.

Angel Hair with Garlic and Olive Oil

Ingredients:

- 12 oz angel hair pasta
- ¼ cup olive oil
- 4 cloves garlic, thinly sliced
- Red pepper flakes (optional)
- Fresh parsley, chopped
- Salt

Instructions:

1. Cook angel hair until al dente.
2. Heat olive oil, gently sauté garlic until golden (don't burn).
3. Add red pepper flakes if using.
4. Toss pasta with garlic oil, season with salt and garnish with parsley.

Ravioli with Spinach and Ricotta

Ingredients:

- 1 package fresh or frozen ravioli (spinach and ricotta filled)
- 2 tbsp butter
- 1 clove garlic, minced
- 1 cup marinara or sage brown butter sauce
- Grated Parmesan

Instructions:

1. Cook ravioli according to package instructions.
2. For butter sauce, melt butter and add garlic and sage, cook briefly.
3. Toss cooked ravioli with sauce or serve with marinara.
4. Top with Parmesan.

Bucatini all'Amatriciana

Ingredients:

- 12 oz bucatini
- 4 oz guanciale or pancetta, diced
- 1 can (14 oz) crushed tomatoes
- ½ cup grated Pecorino Romano
- 1 small onion, chopped
- Red pepper flakes
- Olive oil

Instructions:

1. Cook bucatini until al dente.
2. Sauté guanciale in olive oil until crispy, remove excess fat.
3. Add onion and red pepper flakes, cook until soft.
4. Stir in tomatoes, simmer 15 minutes.
5. Toss pasta with sauce and Pecorino Romano.

Pasta Primavera

Ingredients:

- 12 oz pasta (penne, farfalle, or linguine)
- 1 cup cherry tomatoes, halved
- 1 cup zucchini, sliced
- 1 cup bell peppers, sliced
- 1 cup asparagus, chopped
- 2 cloves garlic, minced
- 3 tbsp olive oil
- Fresh basil or parsley
- Salt and pepper

Instructions:

1. Cook pasta until al dente.
2. Sauté garlic and vegetables in olive oil until tender-crisp.
3. Toss pasta with vegetables, season, and garnish with herbs.

Cannelloni Stuffed with Ricotta and Spinach

Ingredients:

- 12 cannelloni tubes
- 2 cups ricotta cheese
- 1 cup cooked spinach, chopped
- 1 egg
- 2 cups marinara sauce
- 1 cup shredded mozzarella
- Grated Parmesan

Instructions:

1. Mix ricotta, spinach, and egg.
2. Stuff cannelloni with mixture.
3. Place in baking dish, cover with marinara and mozzarella.
4. Bake at 375°F for 30-35 minutes until bubbly and golden.

Lasagne Verde

Ingredients:

- Green lasagna noodles (spinach pasta)
- 2 cups béchamel sauce
- 2 cups shredded mozzarella
- 2 cups ricotta
- 2 cups spinach, sautéed and drained
- 1 cup grated Parmesan

Instructions:

1. Preheat oven to 375°F.
2. Layer noodles, ricotta mixed with spinach, béchamel, mozzarella, and Parmesan.
3. Repeat layers, ending with cheese.
4. Bake 35-40 minutes until golden.

Spaghetti with Meatballs

Ingredients:

- 12 oz spaghetti
- Meatballs (beef/pork mix)
- 2 cups marinara sauce
- Grated Parmesan
- Fresh basil

Instructions:

1. Cook spaghetti until al dente.
2. Brown meatballs in a pan, then simmer in marinara sauce until cooked through.
3. Serve meatballs and sauce over spaghetti.
4. Garnish with Parmesan and basil.

Orecchiette with Sausage and Peppers

Ingredients:

- 12 oz orecchiette
- 1 lb Italian sausage, casings removed
- 1 red bell pepper, sliced
- 1 yellow bell pepper, sliced
- 1 onion, sliced
- 3 cloves garlic, minced
- 2 tbsp olive oil
- Salt, pepper, red pepper flakes (optional)
- Fresh parsley, chopped

Instructions:

1. Cook orecchiette until al dente. Drain and set aside.
2. Heat olive oil, sauté sausage until browned. Remove and set aside.
3. In the same pan, sauté onions, garlic, and bell peppers until softened.
4. Return sausage to the pan, mix with peppers and season.
5. Toss pasta with sausage and peppers, garnish with parsley.

Rigatoni with Sausage and Broccoli

Ingredients:

- 12 oz rigatoni
- 1 lb Italian sausage, crumbled
- 1 head broccoli, cut into florets
- 3 cloves garlic, minced
- 2 tbsp olive oil
- Red pepper flakes
- Grated Parmesan

Instructions:

1. Cook rigatoni and broccoli florets together until al dente. Drain.
2. Sauté sausage and garlic in olive oil until cooked.
3. Toss pasta and broccoli with sausage mixture.
4. Season and top with Parmesan.

Tagliatelle al Tartufo (Tagliatelle with Truffle)

Ingredients:

- 12 oz tagliatelle
- 3 tbsp unsalted butter
- 1-2 tsp truffle oil or shaved truffles
- Salt and pepper
- Grated Parmesan

Instructions:

1. Cook tagliatelle until al dente.
2. Melt butter, toss pasta in butter and truffle oil/shavings.
3. Season and top with Parmesan.

Gemelli with Pesto and Potatoes

Ingredients:

- 12 oz gemelli pasta
- 1 cup pesto sauce
- 2 medium potatoes, peeled and diced
- 2 tbsp olive oil
- Salt and pepper

Instructions:

1. Boil potatoes until tender, then drain.
2. Cook gemelli until al dente, drain.
3. Toss pasta and potatoes with pesto sauce.
4. Season with salt and pepper, drizzle olive oil.

Linguine with Clams

(See previous Linguine alle Vongole recipe)

Rotini with Roasted Vegetables

Ingredients:

- 12 oz rotini
- 1 cup zucchini, diced
- 1 cup bell peppers, diced
- 1 cup cherry tomatoes
- 1 cup eggplant, diced
- 3 tbsp olive oil
- 2 cloves garlic, minced
- Salt, pepper, fresh basil

Instructions:

1. Roast vegetables tossed with olive oil, salt, and pepper at 400°F for 20-25 mins.
2. Cook rotini until al dente.
3. Toss pasta with roasted vegetables and garlic.
4. Garnish with fresh basil.

Capellini with Lemon and Basil

Ingredients:

- 12 oz capellini (angel hair)
- ¼ cup olive oil
- Zest and juice of 1 lemon
- 2 cloves garlic, minced
- Fresh basil, chopped
- Salt and pepper
- Grated Parmesan

Instructions:

1. Cook capellini until al dente.
2. Heat olive oil, lightly sauté garlic.
3. Toss pasta with lemon juice, zest, garlic oil, basil, and Parmesan.
4. Season with salt and pepper.

Manicotti with Meat Sauce

Ingredients:

- 12 manicotti shells
- 2 cups ricotta cheese
- 1 lb ground beef or Italian sausage
- 2 cups marinara sauce
- 1 cup shredded mozzarella
- ½ cup grated Parmesan
- 1 egg
- 2 cloves garlic, minced
- Salt and pepper

Instructions:

1. Cook manicotti shells according to package directions, drain.
2. Brown meat with garlic, drain fat. Mix with marinara sauce.
3. Combine ricotta, egg, salt, and pepper.
4. Stuff shells with ricotta mixture, place in baking dish.
5. Pour meat sauce over manicotti, top with mozzarella and Parmesan.
6. Bake at 375°F for 30-35 minutes.

Penne with Gorgonzola Cream Sauce

Ingredients:

- 12 oz penne
- 4 oz Gorgonzola cheese, crumbled
- 1 cup heavy cream
- 2 tbsp butter
- Salt and pepper
- Chopped walnuts (optional)
- Fresh parsley for garnish

Instructions:

1. Cook penne until al dente. Drain.
2. In a pan, melt butter, add heavy cream and Gorgonzola, stir until cheese melts.
3. Season with salt and pepper.
4. Toss pasta with sauce, garnish with walnuts and parsley.

Spaghetti with Crab and Chili

Ingredients:

- 12 oz spaghetti
- 8 oz fresh crab meat
- 3 cloves garlic, minced
- 1 small red chili, chopped (or red chili flakes)
- 3 tbsp olive oil
- Juice of 1 lemon
- Fresh parsley, chopped
- Salt and pepper

Instructions:

1. Cook spaghetti until al dente. Drain, reserving some pasta water.
2. Heat olive oil, sauté garlic and chili until fragrant.
3. Add crab meat, warm through.
4. Toss pasta into pan, add lemon juice and a splash of reserved water to loosen sauce.
5. Season and garnish with parsley.

Fettuccine with Lobster Sauce

Ingredients:

- 12 oz fettuccine
- 1 lobster tail (cooked, chopped)
- 2 tbsp butter
- 2 cloves garlic, minced
- 1 cup heavy cream
- ½ cup white wine
- 1 tbsp tomato paste
- Salt and pepper
- Fresh parsley

Instructions:

1. Cook fettuccine until al dente. Drain.
2. In a pan, sauté garlic in butter. Add white wine and tomato paste, reduce slightly.
3. Stir in cream and lobster meat, simmer gently.
4. Toss pasta with sauce, season, garnish with parsley.

Lasagna Primavera

Ingredients:

- Lasagna noodles
- 2 cups mixed sautéed vegetables (zucchini, bell peppers, asparagus, peas)
- 2 cups béchamel or white sauce
- 1½ cups ricotta cheese
- 2 cups shredded mozzarella
- ½ cup grated Parmesan

Instructions:

1. Preheat oven to 375°F.
2. Layer noodles, ricotta mixed with vegetables, béchamel, mozzarella, and Parmesan in baking dish.
3. Repeat layers, ending with cheese.
4. Bake 35-40 minutes until golden and bubbly.

Pappardelle with Rabbit Ragù

Ingredients:

- 12 oz pappardelle
- 1 lb rabbit meat, cut into chunks
- 1 onion, chopped
- 2 cloves garlic, minced
- 1 carrot, diced
- 1 celery stalk, diced
- 1 cup red wine
- 1 can crushed tomatoes
- Olive oil, salt, pepper, rosemary

Instructions:

1. Brown rabbit meat in olive oil, set aside.
2. Sauté onion, garlic, carrot, celery until soft.
3. Add rabbit back, pour in wine, reduce.
4. Add tomatoes and rosemary, simmer 1-2 hours until meat tender.
5. Cook pappardelle, toss with ragù.

Pasta Salad with Italian Dressing

Ingredients:

- 12 oz pasta (rotini, penne, or farfalle)
- Cherry tomatoes, halved
- Cucumber, diced
- Black olives, sliced
- Red onion, thinly sliced
- Mozzarella balls or cubes
- Fresh basil
- Italian dressing (olive oil, vinegar, garlic, oregano, salt, pepper)

Instructions:

1. Cook pasta, rinse with cold water, drain.
2. Toss pasta with veggies, cheese, basil, and dressing.
3. Chill before serving.

Ravioli with Sage Butter and Parmesan

Ingredients:

- 1 package fresh or frozen ravioli (any filling)
- 6 tbsp butter
- 8-10 fresh sage leaves
- Grated Parmesan
- Salt and pepper

Instructions:

1. Cook ravioli according to package. Drain.
2. Melt butter, fry sage leaves until crisp and butter browns slightly.
3. Toss ravioli in sage butter.
4. Serve with Parmesan.

Bucatini with Pancetta and Peas

Ingredients:

- 12 oz bucatini
- 4 oz pancetta, diced
- 1 cup peas (fresh or frozen)
- 3 cloves garlic, minced
- 2 tbsp olive oil
- Grated Pecorino Romano
- Salt and pepper

Instructions:

1. Cook bucatini until al dente, adding peas in last 3 minutes. Drain.
2. Sauté pancetta until crispy, add garlic.
3. Toss pasta and peas with pancetta.
4. Season and top with Pecorino Romano.

Spaghetti with Garlic and Breadcrumbs

Ingredients:

- Spaghetti
- Olive oil
- Garlic, sliced
- Breadcrumbs (toasted)
- Red pepper flakes (optional)
- Parsley, chopped
- Salt

Instructions:

1. Cook spaghetti al dente.
2. Sauté garlic in olive oil until golden.
3. Add toasted breadcrumbs, toss.
4. Combine with pasta, season, sprinkle parsley.

Penne with Eggplant and Tomato Sauce

Ingredients:

- Penne
- Eggplant, cubed
- Tomato sauce
- Garlic, minced
- Olive oil
- Basil
- Salt, pepper

Instructions:

1. Cook penne.
2. Sauté eggplant until tender.
3. Add garlic, tomato sauce, simmer.
4. Toss pasta with sauce, garnish basil.

Gnocchi alla Sorrentina

Ingredients:

- Gnocchi
- Tomato sauce
- Mozzarella, diced
- Basil
- Parmesan

Instructions:

1. Cook gnocchi.
2. Toss with warm tomato sauce, mozzarella, basil.
3. Bake 10 min until cheese melts, sprinkle Parmesan.

Cavatappi with Cheddar and Bacon

Ingredients:

- Cavatappi pasta
- Cheddar cheese sauce
- Cooked bacon, crumbled

Instructions:

1. Cook pasta.
2. Mix with cheddar cheese sauce.
3. Stir in bacon, serve hot.

Tagliolini with Lemon and Parmesan

Ingredients:

- Tagliolini
- Lemon zest and juice
- Butter
- Parmesan
- Salt, pepper

Instructions:

1. Cook tagliolini.
2. Toss with butter, lemon zest, juice, and Parmesan.
3. Season and serve.

Tortellini with Creamy Mushroom Sauce

Ingredients:

- Tortellini
- Mushrooms, sliced
- Cream
- Garlic
- Parmesan
- Butter

Instructions:

1. Cook tortellini.
2. Sauté mushrooms, garlic in butter.
3. Add cream, simmer, add Parmesan.
4. Toss pasta in sauce.

Fusilli with Pesto and Pine Nuts

Ingredients:

- Fusilli
- Pesto sauce
- Toasted pine nuts

Instructions:

1. Cook fusilli.
2. Toss with pesto.
3. Sprinkle pine nuts.

Spaghetti with Anchovies and Capers

Ingredients:

- Spaghetti
- Anchovy fillets
- Capers
- Garlic
- Olive oil
- Red pepper flakes

Instructions:

1. Cook spaghetti.
2. Sauté garlic, anchovies, capers in olive oil.
3. Toss pasta, add red pepper flakes.

www.ingramcontent.com/pod-product-compliance
Lightning Source LLC
LaVergne TN
LVHW081324060526
838201LV00055B/2455